Nature watch fish

Steve Parish
KIDS

CONTENTS

What makes a fish?

Fish eye

Fish scales

Fish are incredible animals that mostly live their whole lives underwater. Almost all fish breathe through gills, rather than lungs, and have skin covered in hard scales. They also have special eyes that allow them to see underwater.

Gill slits near a fish's head help it "breathe" underwater. Water passes through a fish's gills as it swims and oxygen in the water is drawn into the fish's bloodstream.

Bamboo shark gills

John dory

Eastern spiny gurnard

Fin fans

Fins are like a fish's arms and are used to steer the fish and help it swim faster. Some fish use their fins like bicycle stands, to "prop" themselves up on the sea floor.

1. BONY FISH

Bony fish make up the biggest fish group and there are many thousands of types. Most of the fish you see if you snorkel will be bony fish. They have teeth-filled jaws, fins, and a hard skeleton covered by scaly skin. But some, such as seahorses, eels and pufferfish, do not look much like fish at all!

Trevally

Seahorse

Porcupinefish

Eel

Unlike bony fish, sharks, rays and stingarees have skeletons of cartilage (the same stuff that makes up your nose tip). This makes sharks light and flexible in the water. They also have rough scales and sharp teeth. Rays are shark relatives that have stinging "barbed" tails.

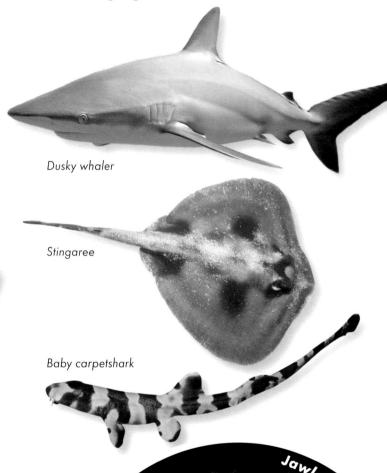

Dusky whaler

Stingaree

Baby carpetshark

Jawless fish

3. JAWLESS FISH

Jawless fish have lived for millions of years but humans rarely see them because they live far down in the ocean's depths. As their name suggests, they have no jaws. Instead they suck up rotting food (called detritus) on the ocean floor with their disc-shaped mouths. Some are so ugly that they have become known as "hagfish".

Fish through the ages

Arandaspis

Fish are amazingly ancient. They were the first animals to have backbones and lived even before the dinosaurs did. Scientists know that jawless fish were the first fish because the fossilised heads of jawless fish found in Australia are hundreds of millions of years old. The most ancient fish known to have lived in Australia was a jawless fish called *Arandaspis*. It was a small fish with an armoured tail, no fins and more than ten paired gills.

Most fish have changed a lot over time, but hagfish have stayed very simple. They have no teeth, no jaws and no eyes because they live in deep, dark water.

Hagfish

Broadnose shark

Placoderm fossil

Fishy fossils

Sharks are the next oldest type of fish, followed by modern bony fish. The first fish with jaws were the placoderms, which are now extinct. Scientists call the time after placoderms became extinct the "Age of Fish" because so many types of fish evolved then.

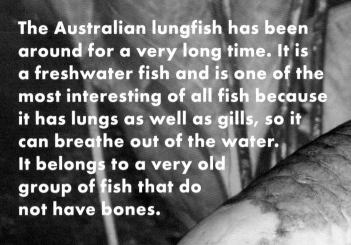

The Australian lungfish has been around for a very long time. It is a freshwater fish and is one of the most interesting of all fish because it has lungs as well as gills, so it can breathe out of the water. It belongs to a very old group of fish that do not have bones.

Australian lungfish

The fish time forgot

Coelacanth

The coelacanth fish, like the lungfish, is often called a "living fossil" because for hundreds of years scientists thought it was extinct. Ancient fossils showed that it lived as long as 400 million years ago. When one was found in 1938, scientists were amazed.

Pink anemonefish

Underwater homes

Fish come in all shapes, sizes and colours and live in many different underwater homes.

Some live on coral and cold water reefs, which are like underwater cities for fish. Others like to hide in seaweeds and seagrass, or make themselves blend in with the colours of the ocean floor.

Many live and swim in groups called "schools". Some larger fish and sharks prefer to live alone in the open ocean.

Moray eel

Butterfly perch

Longnose butterflyfish

Trevally

School for fish

A fish school is very different to a human school, of course. Fish that swim in schools mostly learn how to avoid hungry predators. They are much safer in a group than they would be swimming alone in their watery home.

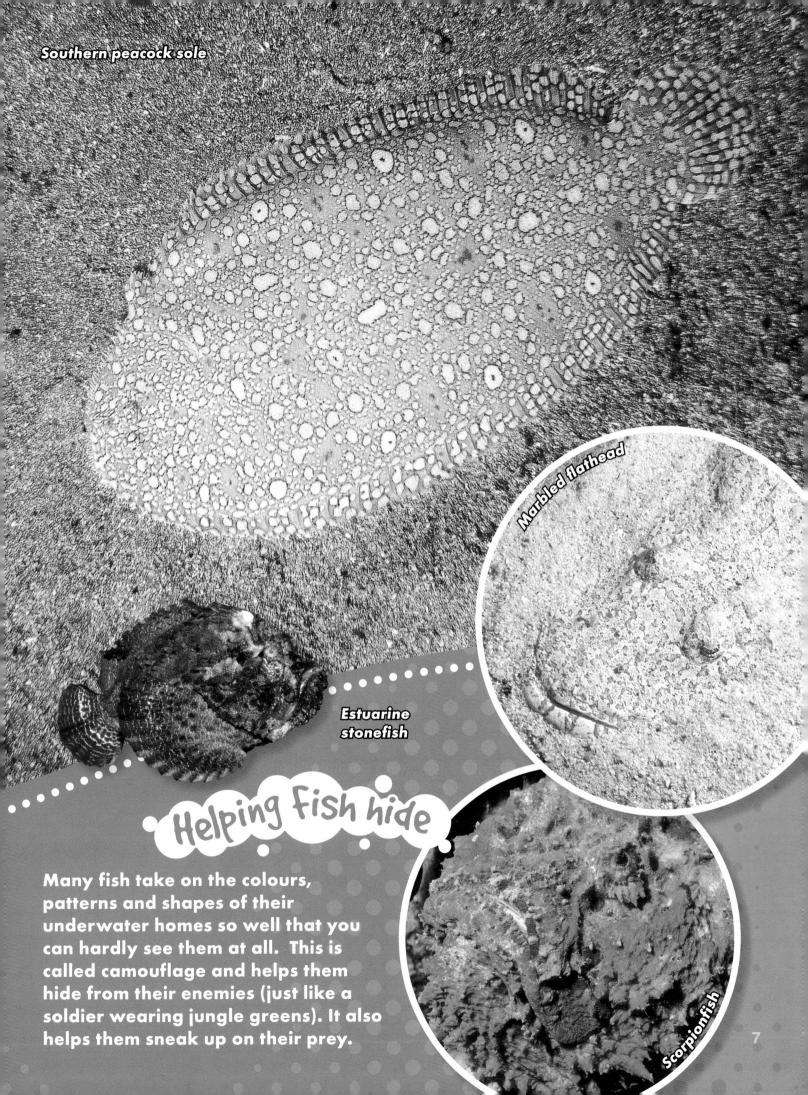

Southern peacock sole

Marbled flathead

Estuarine stonefish

Helping fish hide

Many fish take on the colours, patterns and shapes of their underwater homes so well that you can hardly see them at all. This is called camouflage and helps them hide from their enemies (just like a soldier wearing jungle greens). It also helps them sneak up on their prey.

Scorpionfish

Small fry & fish eggs

Port Jackson shark & eggcase

Most fish lay eggs, but some sharks give birth to live babies. Some fish keep their eggs in their mouths, or in an unusual eggcase or pouch until they hatch. Some fish can even change from male to female to lay eggs!

Baby Port Jackson sharks hatch from an odd-looking eggcase that looks just like a spiral shell.

Tasselled anglerfish hatch from eggs. This picture shows them growing bigger inside the egg, feeding off the yolk in the egg sac.

Fish eggs

Orangelined cardinalfish

Don't swallow, Dad!

Cardinalfish are known as "mouth brooders" because the father cardinalfish keeps eggs inside his mouth until they hatch. Strangely enough, the eggs are very safe in the dad's mouth as it means other marine predators that feast on fish eggs can't get to them.

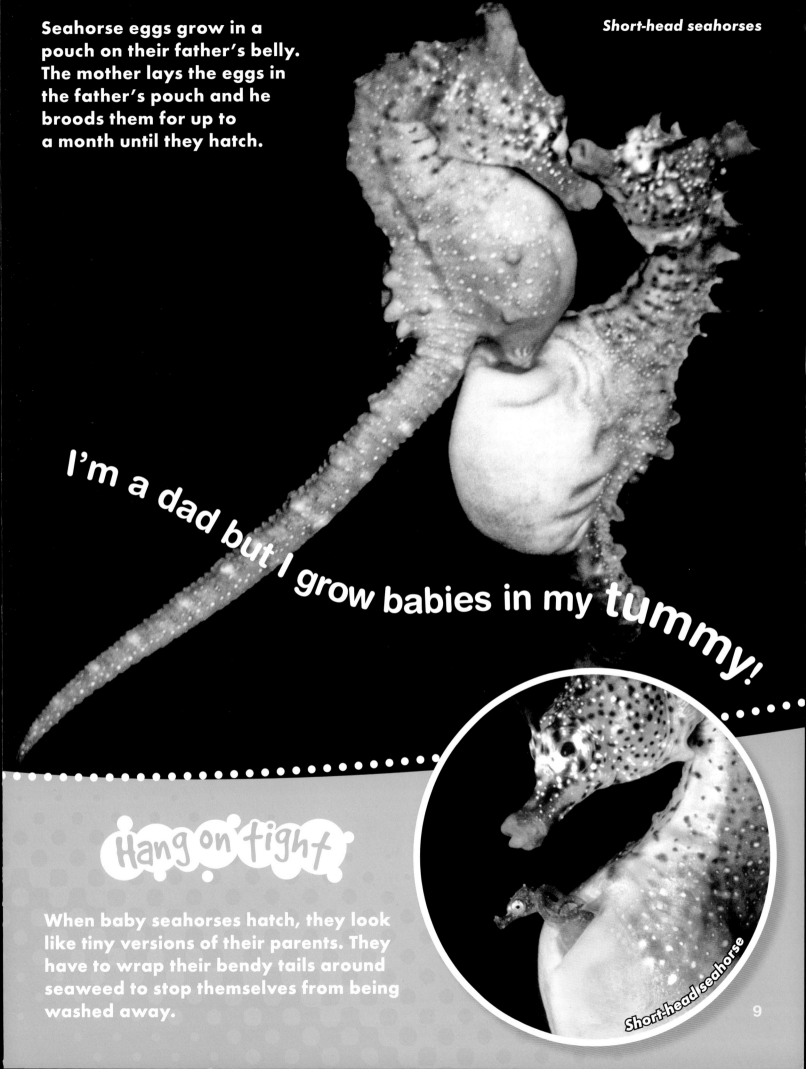

Seahorse eggs grow in a pouch on their father's belly. The mother lays the eggs in the father's pouch and he broods them for up to a month until they hatch.

I'm a dad but I grow babies in my tummy!

Hang on tight

When baby seahorses hatch, they look like tiny versions of their parents. They have to wrap their bendy tails around seaweed to stop themselves from being washed away.

Short-head seahorse

Fish talk

Scalloped hammerhead

Fish communicate using sound, scent, colour, movement and electrical signals, and they can be rather noisy underwater. They may grunt, squeak or make other sounds to attract a mate. A fish's colours and patterns also "talk" to other fish. Bright colours, patterns or spines may say, "Don't eat me, I'm poisonous!" Some fish that live in deep water even glow in the dark, which is also a type of communication.

A school of trevally may follow a shark, which can protect them from other predators and let them pick up scraps left over when the shark feeds. The shark's body language helps tell the trevally when the shark is calm and will not eat them. When sharks hunt, their bodies stiffen and they may hold the fins on their sides differently, which lets the trevally know it is not safe to hang around.

HUFF & PUFF

Fish can also tell a predator to back off by making themselves look bigger or scarier than they really are. If threatened, porcupinefish and pufferfish gulp air or water to blow their bodies up and frighten attackers. Other fish may change colour, wave their fins around, or nip at attackers.

Porcupinefish

Reticulated butterflyfish

When butterflyfish find a mate, they often flutter their fins and move about in a kind of dance. This is their way of telling each other how excited they are to have found a partner.

Whitetip reef shark & trevally

Other fish know when I'm hungry!

Please clean me...

Fish don't have hands to pick off pesky parasites or scabby skin. Instead, they allow cleanerfish, which eat dead skin or parasites, to do it for them. A fish stays still with its mouth open and its fins spread to tell the cleanerfish that it wants a clean.

Coral trout & cleanerfish

Sleek & swift

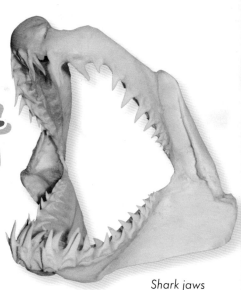

Eagle ray

Shark jaws

Sharks and their relatives, the rays, are very well designed for ocean living. Sharks have streamlined bodies and razor-sharp teeth for devouring prey. Rays come in many sizes and are clever at camouflage, often making themselves almost invisible on the muddy or sandy bottom.

Oceanic whitetip shark

Sharks and rays look very different. Sharks have long, sleek bodies with pointed fins and gill slits on the side of the body. Rays' fins are flattened to give them a round or diamond-like shape and their gill slits are under their bodies.

Many rays and stingarees live on the sea floor. They have eyes on top of their heads, but their mouths are underneath so they can eat shellfish off the bottom.

Bluespotted maskray

Eastern fiddler ray eye

Eye breathing

A ray's gills are under its body, which makes it hard to pass water through the gill slits. Instead, rays have a hole, called a spiracle, near the eye that moves water through the gills.

White shark

I can swim very far, from Africa to Australia.

Tough teeth

Sharks' sharp teeth fall out all the time, about once every week, and are replaced by more straight away. Strangely, although they may have thousands of teeth in their jaws at once, most sharks can't chew. They use their teeth to tear off chunks of fish flesh and swallow it whole instead.

Shark teeth

Port Jackson shark

Prowling the bottom

Epaulette shark

Some sharks look quite unlike the fast, finned sharks you might know. Sea floor sharks include wobbegongs and other odd-looking, patterned sharks that feed on shellfish on the sandy, rocky or muddy bottom.

Zebra shark

The epaulette shark is a small spotted "carpetshark" that lives on coral reefs in Australia's north.

Australia has many types of wobbegong sharks, which hide in shallow water over coral or rocky reefs by day and hunt at night.

Tasselled wobbegong

Digging in the dirt

Elephantfish

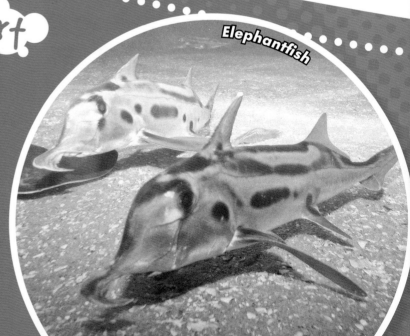

Elephantfish are unusual shark relatives that have a dorsal (or top) fin that can be folded down. They also have only one pair of gill slits and an odd nose that they use like a plough to dig up the seabed, searching for squid, small fish and shellfish. Very sensitive organs on the nose help them feel electrical currents made by moving prey.

Many sharks and rays
that sit on the sea floor
have venomous spines
or barbs for protection.
This stops these slow
swimmers being attacked
by predators from above.
They often live in their own home
territory and if moved they quickly
return to their own "home ground".

Master blaster

A tawny shark can use its mouth like a pump
to suck in prey near the bottom. If attacked,
it can reverse this "mouth pump" to blast out
a jet of water to scare its attacker.

Tawny shark

White shark

The teeth of the reef

Some very special sharks patrol reefs or shallow coastal waters, searching for schools of fish or large reef fish to eat.

These sharks include many types of reef shark and a large group of sharks called whalers. Unlike many other sharks, whalers give birth to live young (rather than lay eggs).

Blacktip reef sharks

Tiger shark

The tiger shark may be the largest predator on tropical reefs. It hunts alone and can also make long-distance trips between reefs to find food.

Bull shark

Not fussy eaters

Bull sharks can be dangerous sharks and have eaten humans. That is mostly because they like to swim in shallow coastal waters, which is where humans also like to swim. Most attacks happen because bull sharks will chomp at almost anything, including other sharks, dolphins and turtles.

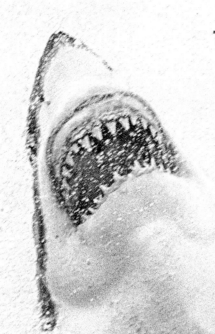

White shark

The white shark (or great white) is a very good hunter. It prowls shallow waters just off shore and can leap high in the air after prey that tries to escape its jaws. It is also the only shark that can move its upper jaws to saw at or "chew" prey. White sharks will even take a bite out of large whales and marine turtles.

I am the mightiest of all sharks!

Head like a hammer

Great hammerhead

It might look funny, but the great hammerhead's long head helps it find prey. The broad head has rows of sensory organs that can "feel" prey in the water and help this shark find food.

17

Long-distance swimmers

Oceanic whitetip

Scalloped hammerhead pup

Some sharks are incredible swimmers that can travel a long way in the open ocean. These sharks are often caught by trawlers out in the high seas and can then be killed and sold as "flake" in fish and chip shops.

Scalloped hammerheads live in deep water and females only come into the shallow reef waters to give birth to their live "pups" (baby sharks).

Dusky whalers grow very slowly and may take 20 years to be fully grown. As they get bigger, they move into deeper northern waters.

Dusky whaler

Basking shark

Mighty mouth

Basking sharks are also known as sunfish because they like to bask, or sunbake, in the sun on the ocean's surface. They are weird-looking sharks with huge mouths but tiny little teeth. The harmless basking shark opens wide its gaping mouth and filters plankton and krill from the water.

The blue shark is the most common shark in the ocean because a female can have up to 40 shark pups at once. They are very thin and streamlined, but are slow swimmers. Because they swim so slowly, they don't use as much energy as other sharks do so they do not have to eat every day.

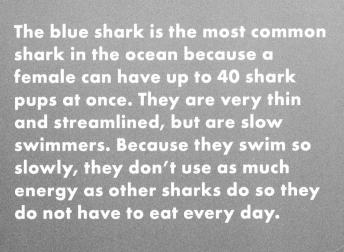

Blue shark

I am a graceful, slow swimmer.

Teeth like daggers

Shortfin mako sharks like warm water out in the open, so they rarely go down very deep. They have ragged, dagger-like teeth that show all the time, even when the shark's mouth is closed. Their teeth are perfect for snagging and tearing up struggling prey. They are believed to be the fastest sharks of all.

Shortfin mako

19

Strange sharks & rays

Shark ray

Rays come in many shapes and sizes, but there are also some "shark rays" that have a few of the features of sharks and some of the features of rays. The one thing that makes rays different from sharks is that rays have gills underneath their bodies.

Shovelnose rays are also known as "guitarfish" because of the shape of their bodies. They have tails and dorsal fins like a shark's, but a head like a ray's.

Eastern shovelnose ray

Fiddler ray (top)

Fiddler ray (underside)

A ray's mouth and gills are underneath its body. Shark rays have their gills on the top or side.

Fiddler rays, unlike true stingrays and stingarees, have no barbs or spines and are harmless to humans.

Ocean angels

The Australian angelshark is a sneaky shark that looks like a ray and likes to lie on the sandy ocean floor. It half buries itself on the sandy sea bottom, from where it can leap up to snatch fish, squid, crabs and shrimps.

Australian angelshark

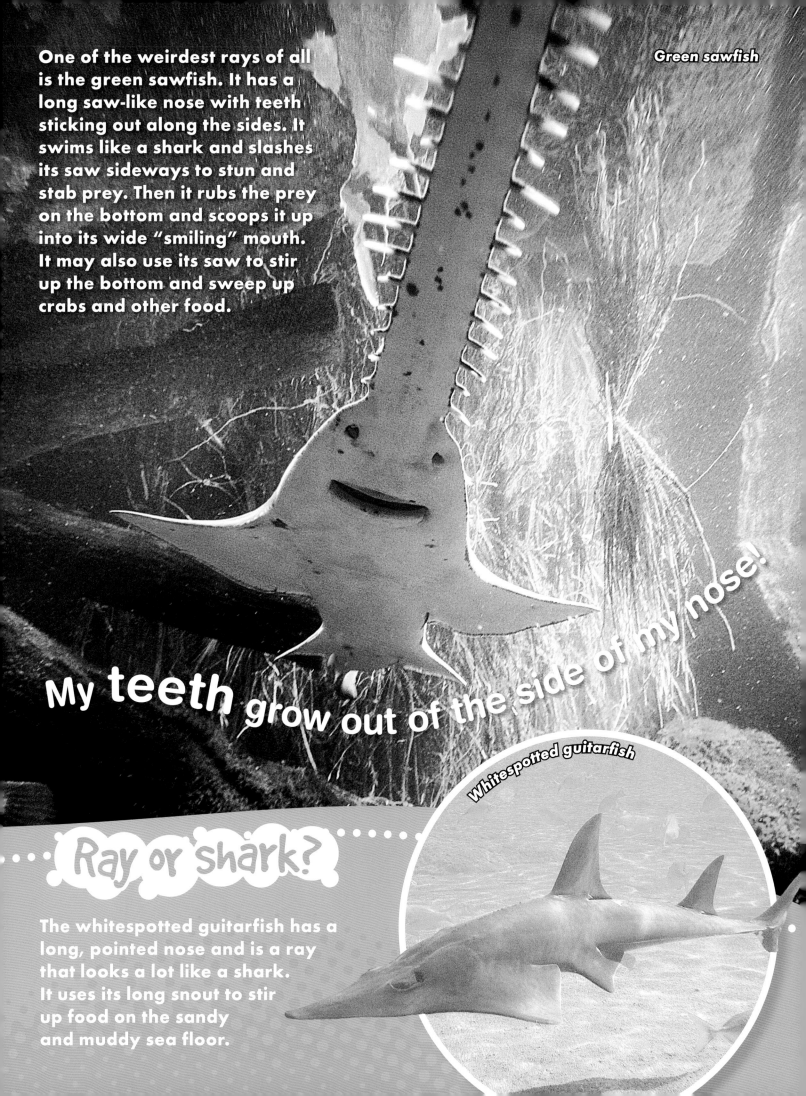

One of the weirdest rays of all is the green sawfish. It has a long saw-like nose with teeth sticking out along the sides. It swims like a shark and slashes its saw sideways to stun and stab prey. Then it rubs the prey on the bottom and scoops it up into its wide "smiling" mouth. It may also use its saw to stir up the bottom and sweep up crabs and other food.

Green sawfish

My **teeth** grow out of the side of my nose!

Whitespotted guitarfish

Ray or shark?

The whitespotted guitarfish has a long, pointed nose and is a ray that looks a lot like a shark. It uses its long snout to stir up food on the sandy and muddy sea floor.

"Flying" through the sea

Stingrays and stingarees are rays that have barbed, venomous tails. They move by "flapping" their broad wing-like fins and spend a lot of time resting on the bottom of the ocean.

Stingrays can grow very large. While they may have many colours and patterns on top of their bodies, their undersides are mostly white.

A venom gland at the base of a stingray's tail can cause a painful wound if the stingray is stepped on or attacked.

Sparsely-spotted stingaree

A stingray's underside

Stingray barb

Divers in a tank at Melbourne Aquarium

Are they dangerous?

It is true that some people have been killed by stingrays, but these unlucky accidents are very rare. A lash from a stingray's barb can hurt, but it is not deadly. Most stingrays and stingarees are quick to avoid humans and sting only if they are disturbed or annoyed.

Blue-spotted fantail stingray

The bright blue spots of the blue-spotted fantail stingray help it camouflage in the dappled ocean, but also look a little like the markings of the blue-ringed octopus. These flashy large stingrays rarely hide in the sand like their relatives do, so their spots may help warn other marine creatures to stay away.

My bright colours warn that I'm venomous.

Coffin ray

Shock & awe

The coffin ray does not need a stinger — it can shock a predator instead. This awesome ray is able to "zap" its prey or attackers with an electric shock! The shock is not deadly but it can give you a big fright.

23

Graceful gliders

Manta ray

The largest of the rays are manta rays and eagle rays. The manta ray is the biggest and is found in waters off many countries around the world. They can have a "fin span" wider than many cars are long. Unlike stingrays, mantas have no venomous barbs.

The long flaps at the front of the manta ray's head help funnel water into the ray's mouth when it feeds. When it swims, it pulls the flaps together to streamline itself.

Manta rays are very graceful in the water, especially when you think that they are large and very heavy. A single manta ray can weigh more than a medium-sized truck!

Smoothtail mobula ray

Jumping for joy

It is amazing to see a huge manta ray or a mobula ray leap right out of the water. Scientists think they may do this to avoid sharks, to communicate with other rays (the slap of re-entry is very loud), to shake parasites off their skin, or just because they enjoy it.

Manta ray

Manta rays are able to swim long distances, even across oceans, but they mostly stay in the same place and migrate (or move) between feeding grounds at certain times of year.

I like to leap out of the waves!

Manta ray

Southern eagle ray

An eagle's beak

Eagle rays have a more pointed snout than manta rays. It looks a bit like a bird's beak. They also have stingers and some, like the southern eagle ray, sit on the bottom so are more speckled.

25

Gentle giants

The enormous whale shark is the largest fish in the ocean. It is a shark not a whale, although it can grow up to 18 metres long, almost as long as two school buses! These huge fish are gentle giants that eat only tiny fish and krill.

Each whale shark's pattern of spots and stripes is different, just like your fingerprints are unlike anyone else's. Scientists have been able to use photographs of whale sharks taken by divers and tourists to study whale sharks' migrations — all by looking at their body patterns!

Whale shark

A monster mouth

Whale sharks gulp in 10 to 20 mouthfuls of water every minute to filter out the tiny plankton they live on. Of course, it takes a huge amount of krill and plankton to keep them full, so they may "filter feed" on billions of little fish and shrimp each day.

I can live for more than 100 years!

Young male whale sharks visit Ningaloo Reef in Western Australia between March and July each year. Divers there are able to swim with these gentle sharks in total safety.

free riders

Suckerfish or remoras latch on to large fish, like the whale shark, using a sucker near their first fin. In this way they get a free ride around the ocean in safety and may also feed on the poo of the bigger fish.

Remora

The biggest fish group

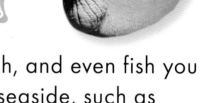

Moray eel

Female shaw's cowfish

Seahorses, eels, scorpionfish, and even fish you may have caught at the seaside, such as bream, are all bony fish.

While they all have bony skeletons, gills and scales, few of their other features are alike! Some are sleek and snake-like. Some have horns, spines or humps. Others have long thin noses for slurping up food.

Bony fish also live in many different habitats. Some live in rock pools, others prefer to hide in seaweed or coral and others spend their lives swimming in schools in the open ocean.

Potbelly seahorse

Longnose butterflyfish

Beneath the scales

If you have ever eaten fish, you will know that you need to watch out for bones. All bony fish have a spine and a skeleton that protects their internal (or inside) organs. Their only limbs are their fins and tail.

Bony fish skeleton

28

Many bony fish swim in large schools, which helps them find safety in numbers. Small fish like blennies and bullseyes, and even very large fish like tuna, swim in schools.

School of black bullseye

Common lionfish

Lures, spines & spikes

Some bony fish have spines, whisker-like barbels, or dangling "lures" coming off their bodies. These may be for protection, to help them blend in with their environment, or to trick prey into coming closer.

Eel catfish

Sand-sifting mud grubbers

Many types of fish survive by eating rotting food, seaweed or small animals on the muddy, sandy or rocky sea floor. Thick, sensitive lips or fleshy barbels help them find food.

Goatfish and catfish have dangling bits of flesh called barbels hanging from their lips. They wiggle their barbels in the sand to sense small invertebrates, then snap them up.

Striped catfish

Goatfish

Morwong

Crab crunchers

Thicklip wrasse

Thicklip wrasse

Thicklip wrasses and morwongs use their lips to feel about in the sand and mud for animals like crabs, prawns, shellfish and other small marine creatures. They suck in food along with sand and shell grit. Any waste is then filtered back out through the gills.

Gurnards are colourful bottom feeders that partly bury themselves in the soft sea floor. They use their pectoral (or front) fins like arms to walk on the bottom or stir up the sand and mud. Their brightly coloured fins and large coloured spots, which look like false eyes, help scare and confuse their attackers.

Butterfly gurnard

Butterfly gurnard

I use my fins to "**walk**" along the bottom.

free for all

Sometimes many fish might feast on the same prey, especially if it is injured or dead and decaying, making it easy pickings. Here, comb wrasse, moon wrasse and mado are eating a sea urchin.

A fish feeding frenzy

Pink clingfish

Still & patient tricksters

Many fish find that patience and camouflage are the best ways to catch food. They have colours or patterns that help them hide in or on coral, in the weeds, or on the bottom. When prey comes close, they pounce.

Brown sabretooth blenny

Tiny blennies hide among coral. They may look harmless but they have sharp, sabre-like lower teeth that can shoot venom into prey or predators.

Like gurnards, hawkfish use their pectoral fins to prop themselves up. They sit on "lookouts" or outcrops on the bottom and ambush small fish, shrimps and prawns.

Prickly anglerfish

Blotched hawkfish

Striate anglerfish

Lured in

Anglerfish "fish" for their dinner. A long piece of dorsal fin sits forward over the anglerfish's mouth, dangling like a lure with a worm-like tip. They sit very still and wiggle the lure to attract prey, which they suck in rapidly.

I lie in wait on the rocky bottom...

Scorpionfish come in many colours and patterns that help them blend into the jagged corals of reefs or the stony sea floor. They have huge heads and upward turned mouths for snatching up unlucky prey.

As still as a stone

Stonefish are the deadliest fish in the world, but they are so well hidden when resting on the bottom that they mostly go unseen. If accidentally stepped on, thirteen sharp and venomous spines along the stonefish's back can pierce the skin and cause great pain or even death to humans.

Estuarine stonefish

33

Coral reef hunters

Squirrelfish

Flashlightfish

Flashlightfish

Coral reefs are very complex habitats made up of many food webs. Each food web can include many carnivorous fish that patrol the reef looking for prey. Whether large or small, these fish send others scattering in their wake.

Soldierfish and squirrelfish are big-eyed, night-hunting predators of crabs and other invertebrate sea creatures that live on the sea floor. Soldierfish get their name from their habit of swimming in large schools that look a little like soldiers on parade.

One amazing reef fish is the flashlightfish. It hides in dark nooks and caves by day and hunts at night, using light-producing organs in its head to light up the reef in search of prey (just like a security guard using a flashlight).

Trumpetfish

Trumpetfish

Tricky trumpetfish

Bright yellow trumpetfish (above) can change their colours to blend in with other fish. They swim close to a school of other fish, as if "piggy-backing", and sneak up on prey. The trumpetfish (above left) has made itself look silver to blend in with Moses snapper.

Moses snapper

34

Lionfish, with their stripes, venomous spines and wavy fins, don't look very much like lions at all, but they are fierce reef predators of fish and shrimps. They flatten their long pectoral fins out to the sides to help "herd" their prey into a corner.

Prowling for prey

The barramundi cod is not related to the freshwater barramundi, although it gets its name for the similar shape of its head and mouth. This large, spotted fish is a bottom-living hunter of small reef fish.

Barramundi cod

High-speed hunters

The vast blue of the open ocean is patrolled by some very successful fish with very large teeth. Some hunt alone, but many swim in large, fast-moving schools that cause panic among smaller fish.

The great barracuda is a fearsome fish that can grow as long as a small car. It cruises the oceans alone, often rather slowly, but it can attack at lightning speed — even tearing its prey apart when it hits.

Although the great barracuda likes to swim solo, its smaller cousin, the blackfin barracuda, forms hunting schools that prey on smaller fish. This hungry mob will even attack and eat smaller fish of their own kind.

Mackerel

Holy mackerel!

Mackerel are very fast fish that swim in large schools in the open ocean. Their sleek, slim bodies help them speed through the water to gobble up slower fish.

36

Blackfin barracuda

Great barracuda

I am a fast and deadly hunter!

White trevally

Golden trevally

forked means fast

Trevallies are also fast-swimming fish that live in schools. Most open-ocean fish have forked tails, which helps strengthen the base of the tail to give them more speed when swimming.

Dick's damsel

Foxface rabbitfish

Plant pickers

Not all fish feed on other animals — some are herbivores, which is another word for vegetarians. Many plants grow in the ocean, including seaweeds, seagrasses and algae that grows on rocks and corals. These ocean plants all provide food for vegetarian fish.

Dick's damsels even grow their own gardens! They chase other fish, crabs or marine animals from their patch of red and green algae and carefully tend and "mow" their lawn to make sure plenty of fresh algae grows.

Onespot puller

Onespot pullers are related to Dick's damsels and also like to peck and "pull" at algae and seaweed on the bottom. This one is protecting its eggs on the sea floor.

Wrasse

Sea sleeping

Fish can't close their eyes, so I bet you're wondering how they sleep. Many just go into a restful state on the bottom (with their eyes open). Some, like sharks, which must swim all the time so they can breathe through their gills, may not sleep at all.

Whitespotted rabbitfish

Algae is not easy for a fish's stomach to process (or digest) and is very low in nutrients and energy. Because of this, parrotfish must graze almost all of the time to stay alive. They also have a lot of bacteria in their stomachs to help them break down the algae.

Bluebanded parrotfish

Parrotfish teeth

Green moon wrasse

Coral Crunchers

Parrotfish have been named for their beak-like fused (joined) teeth, which look like a parrot's beak. They use their teeth to scrape algae off dead coral. They also crunch up the coral, which they later poo out as fine white sand.

Slurpers & suckers

Just as elephants can slurp up water using their trunks, so can some sea animals. Seahorses, seadragons and pipefish all have long combined noses and mouths that are perfect for sucking up tiny marine animals called plankton.

Seahorses

Ghostpipefish

White-faced pipefish

Seahorses, seadragons and pipefish float along in seaweeds or currents and "vacuum" up passing prey that drift by. The seahorse's curly tail anchors it to seaweed in strong currents. Ghostpipefish have more fan-like fins and look like seaweed.

A slurpy worm?

Some pipefish look more like worms than like fish and have no fins at all. They live in shallow water and rely on camouflage for protection. These pipefish wriggle along the bottom, moving like worms and slurping up tiny crabs and shrimps.

Leafy seadragons

We are very hard to spot in seaweed.

Leafy seadragons are very slow swimmers. Luckily, they look almost exactly like the seaweeds they hide among, so many predators overlook them.

Dragons in the deep

With weed-shaped fins and a well-camouflaged body, the weedy seadragon can be very hard to spot when near the sea floor. Baby seadragons hatch from eggs on the father's tail and look just like their parents.

Weedy seadragons

41

Picking at food

Common cleanerfish

Some small fish pick plankton from the water or use their well-adapted snouts to pluck food out from between corals or rocks. Others poke their snouts into coral to pick at mucus (a slimy, slippery covering).

Hulafish

Hulafish are small colourful fish that search the bottom for plankton animals, crabs or shrimps. They are named hulafish because of the way they wriggle their bodies when they swim, just like someone hula dancing.

Garden eels

Garden eels are plankton feeders that stretch up from their burrows like a forest, bobbing and weaving as they pluck plankton from the water.

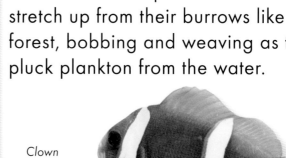

Clown anemonefish

Clown anemonefish

Clowning around

Clown anemonefish make their homes among the tentacles of sea anemones. They feed on small animals trapped by the mucus on the surface of the anemone and also in the open water surrounding the anemone. If danger approaches, they dart in among the anemone's stinging tentacles.

Basslets are beautiful, colourful little fish that are common on coral reefs. They have small mouths and tiny teeth, and suck up plankton from the water. Males and females are different colours, but all basslets start out as females and change into males when they get older!

Fairy basslets

Fairy basslets & damselfish

Perfect for picking

The beaked coralfish is a coral picker that pokes its thin snout-like mouth into tiny nooks and crannies. Cleanerfish also have snouts that are perfect for picking and they use them to pick tiny parasites off the scales of coralfish.

Beaked coralfish

Longnose butterflyfish

Seaweed scrapers

Beautiful butterflyfish flit among coral reefs. Some have pointed mouths filled with fine comb-like teeth that they use to scrape mucus off the coral. Others poke their long "beaks" into coral to seek out and snap up small crabs and prawns.

The eye-like spots on the back of teardrop butterflyfish are called ocelli, which means "little eyes". They make a butterflyfish look bigger than it really is, which scares predators away. Ocelli also trick predators into thinking the fish's head is at the back of its body, so the predator attacks the fish's back, not its head.

Saddle butterflyfish

Teardrop butterflyfish

Scribbled angelfish

Truncate coralfish

We stick together

Many butterflyfish keep the same partner for life and even swim and feed in pairs. When it comes time to make baby longelfish, the female releases clouds of eggs into the water. After being fertilised by the male, the eggs drift off on the current and hatch elsewhere.

Bannerfish are related to butterflyfish and also prefer the warm waters of the Great Barrier Reef. They feed on coral polyps (the tiny animals that make coral), algae and small crustaceans.

Singular bannerfish

My fins stream out like banners as I swim.

Changing Colour

Many angelfish and butterflyfish look very different to their parents when they are young. Young fish may have very complex lines and circular patterns in blue, black and white.

Adult emperor angelfish (top) & young

Looking after fish

Potato cod

Just like many land animals, fish need our help to survive. Sharks are at the top of the ocean food chain, but even they get caught and eaten by humans and many sharks are endangered. Other fish, such as coral pickers and reef fish, are at risk from global warming, which threatens to destroy their reef habitat. We have to look after our oceans to keep fish species alive.

Displays at aquariums help us learn how we might conserve fish. Many people enjoy fishing, but it is important not to catch more fish than you are allowed to (called bag limits).

Visiting aquariums helps you to learn about fish

Stick to bag limits

Threadfin butterflyfish

Leave fish in their habitat

Care for the oceans

Some people try to catch fish to put in tanks or aquariums, but it is important to remember that all fish are part of a circle of life in the ocean. Removing fish from the ocean can upset the natural balance of marine habitats.

Scientists who study fish are called marine biologists. They often dive down to photograph fish underwater. You can learn a lot about the behaviour of fish by snorkelling with your parents, but take care that you try not to disturb the fish you are watching.

Potato cod

Bumphead parrotfish

Vanishing giants

Big fish like wrasse, cod and grouper take years to grow old enough to make babies. Some of these huge fish are on the brink of extinction because people catch them for sport.

Eastern blue grouper

ABSORB To take into the body through the skin or bloodstream.

AMBUSH To attack by surprise.

BREED To produce young that can later go on to have their own babies with members of the same species.

BROOD To keep eggs warm until they hatch.

CAMOUFLAGE When an animal's colour helps it blend in with the background.

DAPPLED Having spots of different colours or shades.

DEVOURING To swallow or eat greedily.

ENDANGERED At risk of becoming extinct.

EVOLVE Changes to an animal or species over time that help it survive in its environment.

EXTINCT When all individuals of a species are dead.

GAPING Wide open.

GILL SLITS Small slits that fish breathe through by passing water through the body and absorbing oxygen.

HABITAT The place where an animal or plant lives or grows.

HERBIVORE An animal that eats plants (a vegetarian animal).

INVERTEBRATES Animals that do not have a backbone or spinal cord in their bodies.

KRILL Tiny shrimp-like animals.

LURE A flap or tassel on a fish that may attract prey.

MARINE Relating to the sea.

MUCUS A slimy substance produced by some animals.

OCELLI Dark spots that look like eyes and trick predators into thinking an animal is bigger than it really is.

PARASITE An animal or plant that lives on or in another animal (the host) and takes nourishment from it.

PLANKTON Tiny plants and animals that float in seawater and cannot be seen without a microscope.

PREDATOR An animal that hunts and eats animals.

PREY Animals that are hunted and eaten by other animals.

SABRE-LIKE Shaped like a sharp, curved sword.

SPECIES A group of animals that share the same features and can breed together to make babies.

TERRITORY The area occupied by and defended by an animal or group of animals.

TRAWLER A boat with a trawl net used for fishing.

VENOMOUS Having a type of poison that can be injected into another animal to injure or kill it.